A Photographic History Of Lye and Wollescote During The Redevelopment 1950s – 1972

Photographs

Harry Cartwright

Authors

Pat Dunn and Colin Wooldridge

HARRY CARTWRIGHT, PAT DUNN AND COLIN WOOLDRIDGE

Copyright © 2013 Harry Cartwright, Pat Dunn, Colin Wooldridge

All rights reserved.

**ISBN-10:
1492771031
ISBN-13:
978-1492771036**

DEDICATION

To the memory of Harry Cartwright

ACKNOWLEDGMENTS

We would like to express our gratitude to Audrey, Harry's widow and Louise Higgs, Harry Cartwright's daughter, for giving us this opportunity to share Harry's photographs. We would also like to say a special thank you to Tracey Jones for her assistance in preparing the book for publishing. We would also like to thank the staff at Stourbridge Library for their assistance and also Colin McDonald for suggesting the project.

A Brief History of Lye & Wollescote

Lye, Wollescote and Stambermill all bear Anglo Saxon names. They were formerly in the ancient parish of Old Swinford and, before the late nineteenth century re-organisation of local government, under the jurisdiction of Halesowen.

Life in Lye was uneventful with the brief exception of Prince Rupert's activities. He was forced to flee from the Roundheads. Mr Milward of Wollescote Hall hid him down a well until the danger had passed. Mr Milward was rewarded when Charles II returned to rule. Some years later, people from outside the area, such as Huguenots, descended on the Lye Waste. Attracted by the area's wealth of raw materials and the prospect of employment, for example, in the nail making trade, they built themselves crude mud huts. One hundred and three were recorded as being in the area in 1699. They did not mix with the local people who regarded them as lawless trouble makers.

However in 1790, the Netherend Unitarian Minister, Reverend James Scott, was a civilising influence, building a permanent chapel for the residents in 1806. In 1813, Thomas Hill, local industrialist and benefactor, founded the Anglican Church sited between Lye Proper and the Waste, thus allowing the integration of Lye and the Waste to take place. Later various non-conformists built their own places of worship – the Wesleyan Chapel (1818), the Primitive Methodists Chapel (1831), Mount Tabor (1871), Gospel Hall (1884), Bethel Chapel (1890), Salem Chapel (1893) and Hayes Lane Chapel (1896). All of these provided educational opportunities, experience in democratic organization, self expression and self help.

From the 1840s, when the major industry of nail making by hand was ruined by mechanisation and foreign competition, other industries were developed. Thomas Perrins built the first chain making factory on Careless Green in 1770. Smaller vice, anvil, horse shoe, frost cog, spade and shovel works also sprang up. The local fireclay led to the manufacture of plain and ornamental bricks, furnace lining and crucibles. However it was the hollow ware industry which developed as Lye's main industry from the late nineteenth century on and the town became known as "the bucket capital of the world." Plastic ruined this trade in the twentieth century.

Factory discipline, religious influences and a secure income introduced a civilised way of life, meaning old bloodthirsty sports disappeared, to be replaced by football and cricket. In 1866, there were 53 Public Houses for a population of 7000. In 1874 the Temperance Hall was built to counteract drunkenness and to provide civilized entertainment. The "Vic" theatre and cinema opened in 1913 and the very posh Clifton cinema in 1937. The three communities Lye, Wollescote and Stambermill benefitted greatly from the opening of Wollescote Park in 1932, the gift of local industrialist Mr Ernest Stevens.

In 1897, Lye and Wollescote Urban District Council had formed and were tackling such problems as slum clearance, sewage disposal, water supply, new housing, street cleaning and street lighting. It was replaced in 1933 when the area became part of the borough of Stourbridge and in 1974 it was taken over by Dudley Metropolitan Council. Under both of the later councils, much of the area was redeveloped with the loss of historic buildings and traditional neighbourhoods.

Harry Cartwright 1923 – 1972

We are indebted to the widow and daughter of Harry Cartwright for allowing us to use some of Harry's evocative photographs to illustrate the changes in the area in the twentieth century. Harry Cartwright was born on 5th June 1923 in Stourbridge. The family lived in West Street, Stourbridge with his Mother and Sister Mary and Brother Cyril. His father died a few years after his brother was born, leaving his widow to bring up the two brothers and their sister. Harry went to Hill Street School, where he became Head Boy. In his leisure time, he was a member of the scouts, thus making lifetime friends and gaining a love for the outdoor life. When he left School, he worked for Kidderminster Co-Operative Society as an insurance agent. This gave him the opportunity to pursue his hobby of photography as he travelled around the area. He joined Stourbridge Institute Photographic Society, later becoming Secretary then President of the Photographic society. He met his wife, Audrey, at the photographic society and in 1963 they were married and had a daughter Louise in 1968.

He was a life time member of West Street Methodist Church and also was a member of Enville Street Dramatic Society. He also enjoyed gardening. He was also a volunteer fireman with Stourbridge Fire Service for many years. Someone who knew Harry well said the memory which stuck in his mind the most about Harry was hearing the fire siren sounding and seeing Harry tucking his trousers in his cycling clips and peddling down the road towards the fire station. He became a driver for the Meals on Wheels service and delivered hot meals to the elderly once a week.

He has left a wonderful legacy of photographs of the local area including those of Lye and Wollescote before and during the dramatic re-development of the area.

Harry suffered with high blood pressure and sadly on the 19th November 1972 he died of a heart attack.

All the profits from this book will be contributed to the British Heart Foundation in memory of his life.

Photographs of Harry

A Photographic History Of Lye and Wollescote During The Redevelopment 1950s – 1970s

High Street, Lye, 1966. Note the variety of architecture of the shops.

Collins Coaches, High Street, Lye, 1960s. Mr Collins also owned a fruit and vegetable shop next to the garage.

High Street, Lye. The white sided building on the right was originally the Clifton Cinema. It was built in 1937 and was one of the most luxurious cinemas in a wide area. It was then taken over by Woodworths for toy and cycle sales, before becoming a market.

Lye High Street, 1960s looking towards Lye Cross. The row of Victorian shops still stands. Note the grandiose poster advertising Greenwoods Chemist shop.

A Photographic History Of Lye and Wollescote During The Redevelopment 1950s – 1970s

Lye High Street, 1960s. Clinic Drive is on the right. It was formerly called Pig Street as there was a butcher's shop on the left, which had an abattoir at the rear. The building still stands but is no longer a butchers.

Woodcraft DIY, High Street, Lye, 1959. It remains unchanged today and is still in business as an ironmongers and DIY shop. The building was erected in **1866**.

A Photographic History Of Lye and Wollescote During The Redevelopment 1950s – 1970s

Lye Cross, 1950's. The Rose and Crown was known as the Mercia because all around the bar was a brass foot rail, similar to those in the old Western movies. The 'Merica' Bar on the left has been replaced by modern shops. The bow fronted building just past it was the Institute which has since been demolished. The Victorian buildings on the left in the distance are still there. The Spire on the Church was removed in 1985.

High Street, Lye. Opposite to where the Clifton Cinema was. Love Lane is on the left. Beaumont's sweet shop is the first shop. Typewriter and Equipment is the second shop. Next to that was Slater and Hughes furniture shop. Then Pharaoh Adams' Butchers and Collins' Coaches.

Lye Institute, High St, Lye. The Working Men's Institute usually called the Stute was built in 1856 and was the scene of serious rioting in 1874, leading eventually to Parliamentary elections undergoing considerable alterations circa 1901. It closed down in 1960 and the site is now occupied by a bank.

Congregational Chapel, High Street, Lye, 1966. The Chapel first opened in 1827. It was also called Mount Sion or "Woods" Chapel after a Lye industrialist who financed it. It is now a Mosque.

A Photographic History Of Lye and Wollescote During The Redevelopment 1950s – 1970s

Corner of Clinic Drive and High Street. Clinic Drive was originally called Pig Street because the butcher who had a shop on the opposite corner to this shop had an abattoir in the street. It was renamed Clinic Drive when the Clinic was built at the end of the Street in Orchard Lane.

Corner of High Street and Chapel Street. The buildings shown from left to right are Collin's Coaches and Collins' Fruit and Vegetable shop. The Bell Public House and the old bank building, which later served as the Urban District Council offices, a solicitors and a dentist.

High Street, Lye, 1966. Little wonder there was demand for a by-pass with a volume of traffic such as this. Note the prestigious Rhodes buildings built c1900, designed by Owen Freeman, manager of George King Harrison's brickworks, for local industrialist Mr Rhodes.

Lye High Street by Worton's shop, 1967. On the extreme left is the forecourt of the Congregational Chapel. Below it is the drapery shop that once belonged to the highly respected Mr J T Worton, who was a prominent member of the Primitive Methodist Chapel and for many years he was Lye's representative on Worcestershire County Council in the nineteenth century.

Labour Club, 1966. Part of the Congregational Chapel is on the left. The Labour party had a strong following in Lye, a branch was formed in October 1898. However the building has now been demolished and at the time of publication of the book, a Mosque is being built on the land.

A Photographic History Of Lye and Wollescote During The Redevelopment 1950s – 1970s

Lye Library on the corner of Chapel Street and High Street. The original Library was in Alton House, home of the Mobberley family, prominent manufacturers. The house was demolished for the building of the new Library on the site in 1935. Sir Cedric Hardwicke declared it open. Lye ambulance station, with the large doors, is next to it.

A view of Bill Pardoe's glass making works in 1961. The firm was known as Stourbridge Stained Glass Works.

Making mirrors, Church Road, Lye, 1961. William Pardon (born in 1862) was a prominent photographer, who lived at 175 High Street. His son Bill (born 1904) carried on a glass working business behind the premises in Church Road. Here a mirror is being polished to remove scratches.

A Photographic History Of Lye and Wollescote During The Redevelopment 1950s – 1970s

Temporary shops on the corner of Dudley Road in the early 1960's. Hidden in the trees at the back of the shops is Lye Cross House, birthplace of the actor Sir Cedric Hardwicke.

Dudley Road, 1967. This was an ancient road, possible a salt road from Dudley to Droitwich. In the photograph, preparations are being made for a road widening scheme. Between the tall buildings and the white building is the way to Lye Railway Station. The line was opened in 1863.

Dudley Road, 1967. Demolition has already started for the widening of the road as can be seen from the ruins of the shops. Orchard Lane is opposite the demolished shop.

The Old Royal Oak, Orchard Lane, Lye. This was on the left of Orchard Lane as you turn into the Ring Road from Dudley Road. It was demolished to make way for the Ring Road.

A Photographic History Of Lye and Wollescote During The Redevelopment 1950s – 1970s

The Dock, 1967. This is a view taken from just above the where the Clifton Cinema was. Already some of the houses in the Dock had been demolished to make way for the ring road.

The Dock before construction of the ring road. The name is an enigma, some say it is derived from horses being taken there to have their tails docked. It joined Vicarage Road to the High Street. Jeavons Bath Works is on the right.

Numbers 11 and 12 The Dock, 1967. The Dock was demolished for a new by-pass. These houses were Victorian and their occupants were obviously very proud of them. An interesting feature is the decorative plaque "Home Sweet Home," which was probably produced in Lye. One of the most unusual sights is the Gnomes sitting on the fence.

A Photographic History Of Lye and Wollescote During The Redevelopment 1950s – 1970s

Name plate on a factory of Jeavons bungalow works in the Dock. In Victorian times, English families living and working in the colonies would buy these for installation in their homes, usually one storied buildings.

The Dock, 1967. A pleasanter view and the curious building on the left could be the wartime public shelter.

The Dock, 1967. Jeavons Bath Factory is on the left and Victorian houses on the right. Notice the neglected state of the footpath and road way. The squat building in the centre of the photograph is possibly a wartime public shelter.

The Dock, 1967. This passageway led from the Dock to Upper High Street. This was a steep and narrow undeveloped track way. On the left appears to be the remains of a mud hut.

The Dock, 1967. Victorian houses are still standing and appear in good condition unlike the roadway.

Upper High St, Lye, 1967. Middle left is Case's ironmongers on the corner of Pump Street.

The Lord Dudley Arms, Upper High Street, Lye. The passage to the left leads to the Dock. On the extreme left is the wall on the Unitarian Chapel. It is said the famous Victorian novelist and hymn writer, Sabine Baring Gould, visited the inn to collect information for his novel Nebo the Nailer, set in Lye, and published in 1902.

A Photographic History Of Lye and Wollescote During The Redevelopment 1950s – 1970s

Unitarian Chapel, Upper High Street, Lye. Known as the Village Church, it was built in 1806 by the Reverend James Scott as a civilizing influence on the lawless inhabitants of the Lye Waste. It was substantially rebuilt in 1861 and the last service was held there in July 1991, but the building still stands. Darby's greengrocer's shop is on the right between the Lord Dudley Arms and the Unitarian Chapel.

Upper High Street, Lye, 1967. Talbot Street is on the left and beyond the corner shop to the right is the Royal Oak Public House. A builder's merchant advert is partly viewable on the right.

Upper High Street, Lye, 1967. The Royal Oak Public House beyond the turning to Talbot Street is viewable on the left. The Avery family shop on the right appears to have closed down. Amazingly, there seems to be little traffic on the road.

Upper High Street, Lye, 1967. The tower of the Unitarian Chapel is left centre complete with steeple and clock commemorating the Queen's Coronation, replacing the original one. Unfortunately it was stolen in broad daylight a few years ago. On the right is Lye Garage Ltd with a selection of cars for sale.

A Photographic History Of Lye and Wollescote During The Redevelopment 1950s – 1970s

Corner of Talbot Street and Upper High Street. A lovely jumble of family shops including a newsagent behind the refuse lorry and a corn merchant.

Hayes Lane. A picturesque scene looking towards Cradley Heath. The white building on the left is the Saltbrook Public House.

Talbot Street, Lye. Skeldings Lane is on the right and Maggie's, a very popular ladies clothes shop is in the centre of the photograph. The Whole area was demolished for re-development in 1960's

Talbot Street, looking towards the flats in Cross Walks. A grim looking study, a Victorian house stands next to a butchers shop. This shop is still standing. The newly built flats on the left were changed and the top story removed and replaced with a conventional roof.

1967, Talbot Street with Pump Street on the right. Note the Victorian corner shop and the row of houses of the same era, also the cobbled pavements.

Talbot Street, 1967. Maggie's dress shop is on the right on the corner of Skeldings Lane. It was an unusual shaped shop. The houses and shops around it are starting to fall into disrepair and awaiting demolition.

Talbot Street leading to Upper High Street.

Talbot Street, 1968. Pem Davies's shop is on the left. Pem and her brother ran two shops. Her brother's shop was on the opposite side of the road on the corner of Star Street.

Talbot Street, 1968. Stan Davies's shop which was a general stores and greengrocers. It occupied the mid eighteen century Star buildings which comprised of the Star Public House, adjacent to the shop which was once a dairy with stabling for horses and other buildings. It fell victim to re-development.

Case's hardware shop on the corner of Pump Street and High Street, Lye, 1967.

Pump Street, Lye, 1967. The street is already starting to show signs of neglect prior to re-development of the area.

A Photographic History Of Lye and Wollescote During The Redevelopment 1950s – 1970s

Skeldings Lane 1967 which ran from Talbot Street to Upper High Street. Fannys Lane is on the right opposite the Hundred House.

Skeldings Lane, 1967. This was an old street that ran from Talbot Street to High Street with another old street Fannys Lane allowing access to Connops Lane. Note the old houses on the right. The Primms Chapel is visible on the left and the spire of Christ Church can be seen in the distance.

Fannys Lane 1967. Victorian houses built straight onto the street, probably safe as little traffic would pass. Note the cobbled area on the right hand side. The lane joined Connops Lane and Skeldings Lane.

Fannys Lane, 1967. Note the Primitive Methodist in the distance. No one knows how the lane acquired its name.

Fannys Lane and Skeldings Lane

Star Street, 1967. This is a short street joining Bank Street and Talbot Street. In Victorian days, a Public House called the Star was situated on the corner of Star Street and Talbot Street. Note the old houses and cobbled pavements.

Connops Lane, Lye, 1967. The Primitive Methodist Sunday School is on the left and Fannys Lane is on the right. The Chapel opened in 1831.

The Primitive Methodist Chapel viewed from Love Lane mid 1960s. The spire of Lye Church can be seen in the distance. General Booth of the Salvation Army conducted a six week mission here in 1863. The building collapsed in 1976.

Love Lane, 1967. Obedience Dickens's shop is on the left. The Primms (the Primitive Methodist) Chapel is still viewable behind the white house and the spire of Christ Church is in the centre of the photograph.

Love Lane, 1967. 1930's built houses can be seen on both sides of the Lane.

View from the back garden in Love Lane towards the Primms Chapel. A labour of love at the back of the house, beautifully landscaped and home to a picturesque street lamp, possibly rescued from the demolition going on all around.

Cross Walks Road, 1967, looking at the Wollescote side of the Road. The Cross Walks Inn is on the right, then Wooldridge's Bakery. Percy Chance's butcher's shop is on the other side of Crabbe Street.

Cross Walks, 1961. A row of Victorian cottages stand on the right. The photograph was taken from where the last mud house stood in Lye. When this was demolished a historic part of Lye's history was gone forever.

Darby's Green grocery and fresh fish shop in Cross Walks. This was a very long established business. The family kept horses at the rear of the property for delivering orders or taking pickers to the family fruit fields in Belbroughton.

A double fronted draper's emporium owned by Mrs Obedience Dickens in Love Lane. This had been the first Co-operative shop to open in Lye or anywhere in the Birmingham area. It was demolished in the 1960's.

The White Horse Public House, Cross Walks. This was demolished in the late 1960's for re-development.

HARRY CARTWRIGHT, PAT DUNN AND COLIN WOOLDRIDGE

Cross Walks viewed from opposite Mount Tabor Chapel. The White Horse is top left by the parked cars and the white fronted building on the right was the Queens Head, known locally as Jack Penn's.

Kitson's shop on the corner of Pope Street, the White Horse is on the nearside left.

The White Horse viewed from Cross Walks by Darby's shop. It was one of 3 pubs in Cross Walks. Note the elegant gas lamp on the corner.

A Photographic History Of Lye and Wollescote During The Redevelopment 1950s – 1970s

Top photo - Kitson's bread delivery in Cross Walks. They were a familiar sight in the area and he was a man held in high regard.

Left photo - Loading bread from the bakery into the delivery cart. Today's health and safety would not approve of the standards.

Interior of Kitson's bakery as stated before, Health and Safety would not be impressed.

Kitson's horse and cart delivering bread in Springfield Avenue. This is an iconic picture of a more leisurely way of life. Perrins Lane is on the horizon. One wonders what the two young cyclists are up to.

Kitson's yard, the grocery shop is on the right and the bakery is on the left behind the white wall belonging to the White Horse. The Bakery would appear to be a very old building compared to the others in the courtyard.

A Photographic History Of Lye and Wollescote During The Redevelopment 1950s – 1970s

Mount Tabor Chapel, Cross Walks, built in 1872. It closed in 1964 and was demolished as part of the re-development scheme. To the right is a roadway leading to Waste Bank.

Back of houses in Cross Walks and Waste Bank 1967. This is an interesting photograph because it illustrates the old type house of Lye and the new offering, provided by re-development, such as modern houses and high rise flats.

Corner of Crabbe Street and Talbot Street. The butcher's shop had been previously been owned for many years by Percy Chance. He produced his own beef at the farm he owned at Belbroughton. They were slaughtered in an abattoir in Crabbe Street at the side of the shop. This photograph was taken after he retired and Mr. F. Oliver took over the shop.

A Photographic History Of Lye and Wollescote During The Redevelopment 1950s – 1970s

View from Cross Walks towards Connops Lane, 1967. Already signs of the destruction to come, but the Anvil Pub is still standing partly obscured by the van and car.

View from Belmont to Summer Street, 1967 This photograph covers a large area bulldozed for re-development, a depressing sight.

View from Cross Walks towards Quarry Bank and Brierley Hill, 1967. A striking picture of massive destruction prior to the re-development. The factory in the foreground is Jonty Perks, beyond which are the few remaining buildings not yet demolished. The high rise flats of Brierley Hill are on the skyline. The five chimneys stacks on the right belong to Round Oak Steel Works.

A Photographic History Of Lye and Wollescote During The Redevelopment 1950s – 1970s

Church Street, Lye. The Temperance Hall which was built in 1874 and later became a cinema, is on the right and the projection room may be seen top right. It closed down in 1950s.

The Temp Cinema, Church Street, Lye prior to demolition. Built as a Temperance Hall in 1874 to discourage Drunkenness. It became a cinema, closing down in the 1950's and being demolished in the 1960's.

HARRY CARTWRIGHT, PAT DUNN AND COLIN WOOLDRIDGE

A beautifully composed photograph showing a view up Church Street. The road rose steeply towards Cross Walks. In the far distance there are signs of the 1960s development of the blocks of flats.

A Photographic History Of Lye and Wollescote During The Redevelopment 1950s – 1970s

The building top right is "Jonty Perks" factory, founded 1861. It was in Church Street Lye and the firm originally produced nails but later specialised in springs, first for horses, then for lorries.

Lower Church Street, Lye. Note the substantial house on the right joining onto Pharaoh Adams' abattoir. Lye Liberal Club's sign is on the left.

Church Street, 1967. In the centre of the photograph is the Salvation Army Citadel built in about 1900, after a branch was founded in Lye in 1881. It was demolished in the massive re-development of the 1960's and members moved to the new HQ on the site of the 1840's National School, which is on the corner of Valley Road and High Street.

Another view of Church Street looking towards Cross Walks.

A Photographic History Of Lye and Wollescote During The Redevelopment 1950s – 1970s

Church Street, showing the Temperance Hall on the left and the Library in the centre of the photograph. The Library was opened by the Lye-born, and internationally acclaimed actor, Sir Cedric Hardwick in 1935.

View from Union Street towards Church Street, 1967. A depressing picture of the horrendous destruction of whole communities for the modernisation of the town. Union Street ran parallel to Church Street and both joined Chapel Street.

Salvation Army Citadel, Church Street, Lye, 1967. The Salvation Army came to Lye in 1881 and was an immediate success. The Citadel was built c1900. When Church Street was demolished, the Salvation Army built a new Citadel on the site of the 1840 National School, on the corner of Valley Road and High Street.

Army Row, 1960. This is a row of terraced houses opposite the Salvation Army Citadel in Church Street, hence its name. The houses appear to be well built and well looked after.

A Photographic History Of Lye and Wollescote During The Redevelopment 1950s – 1970s

View from Church Street to Union Passage, 1967. A depressing view of the destruction over the whole area prior to re-development. A bulldozer can be seen on the left.

Cemetery road with Cross Street on the immediate left and Cross Walks just above.

Cross Street. This joined Cemetery Road to Cross Walks and Union Street was a street off on the left. Note the size of the bricks used to build the houses, which points to being of an early date and probably made locally.

A Photographic History Of Lye and Wollescote During The Redevelopment 1950s – 1970s

Another view of Cross Street, Union Street was opposite the house with the large front window. The houses were demolished in the late 1960's for re-development.

Corner of Belmont Road. Cross Walks Road, is on the left and this was where the last mud hut stood in front of the large dark walled building.

Cemetery Road, Cross Walks is immediate right and the car is turning out of Cross Walks and pointing towards Springfield Avenue which was built in 1931.

Flats being built where Cross Street had stood, 1965. Re-development had begun and the old streets where everyone knew everyone else are beginning to disappear and being replaced by flats.

A Photographic History Of Lye and Wollescote During The Redevelopment 1950s – 1970s

The Bell Inn known as the Top Bell as there was a Bell Public House in High Street, Lye

Pope Street and Belmont Road, Wollescote. The top end of Pope Street, a narrow steep road leading to Cross Walks. Notice the new street lighting.

Looking down Pope Street. The houses on the left are showing signs of dereliction, with the three houses being unoccupied judging by the broken windows. Note the gas lamp with the spire of Christ Church behind it.

View up Pope Street from the rear of the detached house seen in a previous photograph. Note these side streets were still using gas lighting.

A Photographic History Of Lye and Wollescote During The Redevelopment 1950s – 1970s

This view of Pope Street is looking towards Cross Walks. The White building at the bottom is Kitson's shop. Note the brickwork of the house top right which shows it is probably Victorian and the bricks locally made.

A very unusual view taken in Pope Street looking across Waste Bank.

One of the narrow roadways on Waste Bank. The building in the centre of the photograph is the Belmont Chapel.

A Photographic History Of Lye and Wollescote During The Redevelopment 1950s – 1970s

Another view on Waste Bank looking down the roadway shown in the previous photograph.

Nanny Goat Hill, Wollescote. A very steep unmade track till the 1960s. This leads from Springfield Avenue to Monument Avenue. The origin of its name is unknown but can only be speculated upon.

Springfield Avenue, Wollescote, 1961. The road was built in July of 1931 and opened by Mr Ernest Stevens the local Industrialist and benefactor. The houses on the skyline are in Perrins Lane.

Allotments in Springfield Avenue, 1961. Nanny Goat Hill is on the right of the photograph. Allotments are still very popular in the area.

View up Chapel Street with the old Police station on the left. The three storey building behind the police station provided accommodation for single policemen. A new police station was built in the 1930's in Springfield Avenue.

Pouring liquid metal at Samuel Moles' factory in Green Lane, Lye.

The Station Inn, New Farm Road, before its replacement (post 1960) this is now a convenience store.

Grange Lane, Wollescote. A bread man delivering, the open space on the right has since been developed.

A Photographic History Of Lye and Wollescote During The Redevelopment 1950s – 1970s

Hadcroft Brick Works, Grange Lane, Wollescote c1960. Raw materials for brick making were plentiful in the area and were extracted from nearby marl holes. Adjacent to it was a farm.

The Bulls Head, 1960, Pedmore Road, Lye. An interesting photograph as it shows the interior of the old Bulls Head was of a great age. Behind it is the new Bulls Head built in 1960.

A picture of both Bulls Head pubs shown from a different angle, taken at the same time as the previous photograph.

Another view of the new Bulls Head. Green Lane is on the right.

A Photographic History Of Lye and Wollescote During The Redevelopment 1950s – 1970s

Pedmore Road, Lye. On the right is the old toll house by the bend in the road. In the distance on the left is the Hadcroft Brick Works, now demolished. Bricks from this brickyard were used to build the Viaduct between Lye and Stourbridge.

Gallies Garage, Stourbridge Road, Lye. It was a petrol station and demolished in the early 1970's.

Fred Homer hawking his greengrocery in Lower High Street Lye. Higgins factory is on the right.

Another delightful picture of Mr Homer serving a customer. His horse seems to be getting bored.

A Photographic History Of Lye and Wollescote During The Redevelopment 1950s – 1970s

The George Inn, Lower High Street, Lye. The unprepossessing little Public House was on the main road opposite Lye Football ground. It is starting to show signs of neglect.

Milkman with float in Stambermill, 1964. Until quite recent times, horsepower was often seen on local streets. Judging by the contents of his crate, sterilized milk was very popular with customers as fridges were still comparatively rare.

Heart in Hand, Stambermill. This is a much older photograph than the others being taken in the 1930's. It was probably a photograph of a photograph. Note the railway line at the rear right is the GWR Stourbridge Junction to Birmingham route, complete with steam train, freight and signals.

Made in the USA
Charleston, SC
09 February 2014